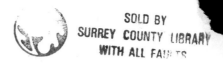

Watching Their Figures

A guide to the Citizen's Charter indicators

Printed in the UK for the Audit Commission at Press-On-Printers, Wandsworth, SW18.
ISBN 011 8861239

London: HMSO

Audit Commission 1994
Cartoons by Rupert Besley
Illustrations by Paul Skone, Design Works.

Contents

PART 3: THE CITIZEN'S CHARTER INDICATORS 1993/94   49

INTRODUCTION

Everyone has the right to know how their money is being spent. In the 1993/94 financial year, local authorities in England and Wales spent about £53 billion raised from government grants, business rates and council tax. That means just over £1,000 was spent for every person in the country.

To show if your money is being well-spent, the Audit Commission has drawn up a set of 'indicators' to measure how well local authorities are doing their job. These indicators give all the information you need to see what standards of service your council is providing and how much they cost. Together with your own experience of your council, they will help you decide whether you are getting a good service. You can compare how well your council is doing now with what they have done in the past. You can also compare the services you get from your council with other similar local authorities.

The indicators show what standards of service the public get in different areas. But they do not always show whether it is harder or dearer to provide certain services in some areas of the country than it is in others. Nor do they show you whether some of the circumstances which affect how councils do their job are beyond their control. We have written this guide for anyone interested in looking at this information in more detail. It explains what the indicators mean and how you can use them to decide whether your council is giving you a good service.

We have drawn up this set of indicators with the help and advice of councils, consumer groups, government departments and others. We wanted to make sure most people would accept the indicators as good measures of how well local authorities are doing their job. Some indicators give information that you can easily compare between authorities because the targets set out are the same. But some local authorities set their own targets and it is not as easy to compare these. So, when looking at the indicators, you will need to decide:

▲ how easy it is to compare the information which local authorities have published; and

▲ whether the information is relevant to you.

Because no two councils are the same, there may be different reasons for the way services are provided in different authorities. This may be due to differences between councils that are beyond their control. It may also be because councils have made different decisions on how to spend money and use resources to meet local needs. There will be a wide range of views on what is 'good performance'. A lot will depend on the values and judgements of members of the public, councillors, and council staff. This guide shows you how all these things may affect both the way services are provided and the performance of those services as shown by the Citizen's Charter indicators.

But the Citizen's Charter indicators do not tell you everything about how well your council is doing its job. Other bodies also have schemes for this, for example, the 'Chartermark' scheme run by the Government's Citizen's Charter Unit. Many local authorities have introduced their own indicators, local charters, and other ideas to improve local services and the way they meet the needs of local people. When you think about how well your council is performing, you should take these into account as well as your own experiences of the council.

This guide does not tell you how you should interpret performance as shown by the Citizen's Charter indicators. Our aim is to give information on the indicators, and on circumstances that may change the way services are delivered.

We have divided this guide into three parts:

Part 1 gives information on performance monitoring and the Citizen's Charter indicators

Part 2 explains how the Citizen's Charter indicators may be used to judge how well a local authority is doing its job, and the special circumstances to take into account.

Part 3 is a list of the Citizen's Charter indicators and information on what they are supposed to measure.

PERFORMANCE MONITORING AND THE CITIZEN'S CHARTER

Background to the Citizen's Charter indicators

Performance monitoring means setting targets and measuring how well these targets are met. This idea is not new. Many public and private sector organisations have used performance monitoring to give information on whether they are using their resources in the best possible way.

Local government started to use performance monitoring in the mid-1980s. As budgets became tighter local authorities and others knew they had to look more carefully at the standard of their services. As part of this move to improve public services, some councils introduced local 'Citizen's Charters', which set out the standards of service the public could expect. This led the councils to draw up ways of measuring their performance. In July 1991, the Government launched a national Citizen's Charter, aimed at improving the quality of services throughout the public sector. And, in March 1992, a law was passed to make sure all local authorities published details of the performance they achieve against a set of indicators. For local authorities in England and Wales, the indicators are laid down by the Audit Commission. For local authorities in Scotland, they are laid down by the Accounts Commission.

In December 1992, the Audit Commission published its first list of indicators for the year 1 April 1993 – 31 March 1994. Local authorities will publish details of their performance in that year, measured against the indicators, in local newspapers. They must do this between April and the end of December 1994. In 1995, we will pull all the information together and show how one local authority compares with another. Exhibit 1 explains this process.

Exhibit 1:   The timetable for publishing the indicators

There are four stages in the process...

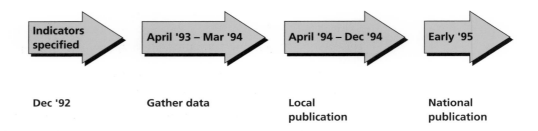

Indicators specified	April '93 – Mar '94	April '94 – Dec '94	Early '95
Dec '92	Gather data	Local publication	National publication

How did the Audit Commission choose its indicators?

We had to decide what information we wanted councils to publish.   The main purpose of the Citizen's Charter indicators is to give the public information about how well their council services are working. But local authorities provide a wide range of services. It is not possible to cover every service, nor would we want to deal with individual services in too much detail. So we asked market research companies to carry out a series of national surveys to find out

▲   what people think is important about the main council services;

▲   what they understand by 'good performance'; and

▲   what sort of information they would like to see published.

The results of these surveys were used to choose the indicators. We also talked to local authorities and nearly 200 other groups whose comments and suggestions were used in putting together a set of draft indicators.

The indicators were chosen to give information which will also be useful to council staff and elected councillors. It will help councils that are not already measuring whether they are providing a good service. They can use the Citizen's Charter indicators to help build their own systems for monitoring performance.

Under the 1992 Local Government Act, the Audit Commission must include indicators of the economy, efficiency and effectiveness of council services. This means there are indicators on how much services cost and also how well those services are working. We have also taken into account:

▲ how useful the information is for making comparisons between different local authorities;

▲ the need to keep down the cost of gathering the information; and

▲ the need to limit the number of indicators which local authorities have to monitor.

Where we have included a service, we have generally set several indicators rather than just one. We have done this for four reasons:

▲ Most council services are made up of several parts. For example, housing departments let homes to tenants, but they also collect rents and carry out repairs. One indicator cannot cover all parts of the service.

▲ There may be more than one way of measuring how well a service is working. One indicator cannot cover the economy, efficiency and effectiveness of a service.

▲ We do not want to encourage councils to divert money or other resources into one part of a service just because its performance is measured by the Citizen's Charter indicators. There is less risk of this if there are several indicators covering different parts of a service.

▲ Some sections of the public may be more interested in certain services and they will want to see a range of indicators which measure in more detail how well these services are working.

We again spoke to consumer groups, local authorities, government departments, professional bodies and other interested parties about our proposals. We took all their comments into account before publishing a final set of indicators in the 'Publication of Information (Standards of Performance) Direction 1992'. A copy of this was sent to all local authorities. Auditors chosen by the Commission will check that the local authorities have the proper systems in place to produce the correct information.

To keep down the cost of gathering the information, we based most of the indicators for 1993/94 on information which local authorities already collect. But this information may not always be the best way of finding out how well a service is working. We will go on trying to find good indicators of performance which we might include in the future. By drawing up these indicators with the help and comments of the public, local authorities and other interested parties, we hope to make them as useful as possible both to the public and to local authorities.

What do the indicators measure?

The Citizen's Charter indicators measure the performance of the main local authority services. For the public, this means trying to work out whether the council provides the services they want without wasting money, and whether those services are of good quality. This still applies where the reasons for doing badly are not entirely the council's fault. Perhaps other organisations have been the cause of poor service or it may be due to circumstances outside the council's control. When local authorities publish their performance against the Citizen's Charter indicators locally, they may want to make clear where they think they are not entirely to blame for a poor service. The indicators are meant to measure how well a service is working against what the public expect of that service. It does not matter whether the council is fully responsible.

The quantity and range of services that a local authority can supply will depend, up to a point, on how much money and other resources – like housing or council buildings – it has. Even the most efficient council cannot keep on adding to its standard of service from a limited pool of resources. The Citizen's Charter indicators include details of what resources the council has as well as how successfully it uses those resources. You should take all these things into account when deciding how good the services you get from your council are.

Some indicators do not directly measure a council's performance. Instead, they give background information that you can use together with indicators of performance to get a full picture of the local services you are getting. Other indicators allow local authorities some freedom in the way they interpret the indicator or the target they use. The indicators may be divided into these four broad groups:

I. Indicators of performance

These include indicators of **efficiency** (for example, the percentage of housing benefit claims dealt with in 14 days) and indicators of **effectiveness** (for example, the percentage of crimes solved by the police). These indicators of performance are also divided into four more groups:

a) Ones where local authorities have to set their own targets and decide how to measure them. (For example, local authorities can decide what targets to set for answering the phone and replying to letters. They can also decide how to measure whether those targets have been met.)

b) Ones where local authorities are told what to measure but no target is set. (For example, local authorities have to say how much waste they have recycled but do not have to set a target.)

c) Ones where local authorities are told what to measure but have to set their own targets. (For example, local authorities must measure how long it takes to carry out a repair and should set their own target times for doing different categories of repair.)

d) Ones where local authorities are told what to measure and what the targets are. (For example, the percentage of householder planning applications decided within eight weeks, where councils have to say how far they have met this target.)

II. Indicators of cost

These help you to decide whether you are getting good value. Although the way a service is carried out may not be directly linked to the money spent on it, as a taxpayer, you have a right to know how much your services cost. Where possible, we have expressed this as cost for each unit of activity or for every person (for example, the amount spent for each pupil) to make comparisons easier. But high costs may not mean the council is doing its job badly. You should use these indicators with the indicators of performance to decide whether you are getting value for money.

III. Indicators of quality

You can use some of the indicators of cost and performance to judge the quality of a service. But we have also included some 'check lists' to help you decide how good a service you are getting. Local authorities must give details of what is included in a service (for example, whether the council takes away garden rubbish free and whether it takes away larger items of rubbish). While most people would agree that the quality of a service is important, it is often difficult to measure. It may be easier to judge quality by looking at a **group** of indicators for a particular service. This is one reason why there are several indicators for most of the services included in the Citizen's Charter indicators.

IV. Indicators providing background information

Some indicators also give information on how much a service is used or about the make-up of the population which the council serves. These indicators help you to link performance to the amount of work that goes in to giving a service (for example, 'the amount of household waste collected' or 'the number of people aged over 65').

In deciding whether you are getting a good service from your local authority, you should take into account what targets it has used and whether you think they are suitable ones. Do they help you judge how well the council is doing its job? You should also consider whether you can compare the standards which have been set locally with those of other local authorities. For example, you will need to decide whether a council that answers 40 per cent of its telephone calls within six seconds is giving a better service than one that answers 80 per cent of its calls within ten seconds.

How do the Citizen's Charter indicators link in with local accountability?

Allowing for some general financial and legal restrictions, there are many decisions which local councillors need to make about the level, quality and cost of services. We know there is a need to give information which can be compared between councils. But this must be balanced with the need to recognise that local councillors must make decisions about which services their councils provide and how to deliver them. That is why some of the indicators are meant to encourage councils to set their own targets. We have asked for performance to be reported against national targets only where other statutory or professional bodies have already set or supported them. And even in these cases, we want the targets to be used as a guide or an example. We are not suggesting they are the only way of judging good performance.

Information on locally agreed targets will be published along with performance measured against the Citizen's Charter indicators. You can use all this information to have your say about how well you think your council is doing its job. You can do this by writing to the council chief executive or to your local councillor, or through the ballot box. But there may be other ways in which councils can help people to use the Citizen's Charter indicators. Members of the public should be given the chance to say whether they think they are getting a good service and what services they want from the council. All councils will be producing detailed information every year and bringing it to the attention of members of the public. They should think about how they can use this to help local people get the services they want. This could be, for example, through local consultative groups where people can say what they think about local services. Or it may be by talking to local consumer groups who represent people with an interest in a particular service. But it may not be enough simply to set up these groups and expect people to take part. It is a new idea to publish performance information on local services with so much detail, and people are not used to taking part in local decision making. Councils will need to encourage people to take part. Local authorities should use the publishing of information as a way of letting local people have a say in the way their council is run.

Which council is responsible for each local service?

All local authorities (except for parish and local town councils, or community councils in Wales) must publish details of how well they have done against the Citizen's Charter indicators. But none of the local authorities on its own provides all the services covered by the Citizen's Charter indicators.

There are three main types of local authority, all with different responsibilities, and so responsible for monitoring performance against different groups of Citizen's Charter indicators.

In metropolitan areas

In the larger towns or cities, council services are run by metropolitan councils or London borough councils. The metropolitan councils are:

Barnsley	Birmingham	Bolton	Bradford
Bury	Calderdale	Coventry	Doncaster
Dudley	Gateshead	Kirklees	Knowsley
Leeds	Liverpool	Manchester	Newcastle-upon-Tyne
North Tyneside	Oldham	Rochdale	Rotherham
St Helens	Salford	Sandwell	Sefton
Sheffield	Solihull	South Tyneside	Stockport
Sunderland	Tameside	Trafford	Wakefield
Walsall	Wigan	Wirral	Wolverhampton

Local authorities in these areas and in London provide all the services covered by the Citizen's Charter indicators except the Metropolitan Police Service in London. The Home Office is directly responsible for the Metropolitan Police. Although the City of London 'Common Council' is responsible for the City of London police, this force does not have to report its performance against the indicators. In all other metropolitan areas, joint boards called police authorities, made up of representatives from the metropolitan councils in each of the old metropolitan county areas, are responsible for the police force in that area. Joint boards, known as fire and civil defence authorities, are also responsible for the fire services in these areas.

Some metropolitan councils and London borough councils do not provide a waste disposal service. Waste disposal authorities in London, Merseyside and Greater Manchester do not have to report their performance against the Citizen's Charter indicators. London borough councils do not control a few other services normally run by local authorities e.g. taxi licensing.

In non–metropolitan areas

In all other areas, two 'tiers' of local government are responsible for council services: county councils and district councils. County councils cover larger areas, usually the same as the county postal area. Within each county council area, there are a number of smaller district councils responsible for a different set of services. District councils are responsible for collecting council tax for both these tiers and passing on the money to pay for county council services through a charge made by the county council. This charge is known as a 'precept'. District councils have no control over the amount of the precept, but must include it in council tax bills.

The county council and the district council may provide the same services in the same area, for example, arts, tourism and museums. Some county council services may be run by district councils within their own areas through 'agency agreements'. In this case, the district is responsible for the day-to-day running of the service. But the county is still responsible for setting standards, deciding how much money can be spent, and making sure people get a good service. This arrangement is often used to maintain roads and street lights.

Table 1 overleaf shows which councils run which services. It also shows which services are covered by Citizen's Charter indicators, and which extra ones will be covered from next year.

Table 1: The main services run by different types of local authority

	Education	Social services	Waste disposal	Public libraries	Trading standards	Highways and rural footpaths	Street lighting	Strategic planning (making a summary plan for the whole area)	Fire	Country parks and tenanted farms	Tourism	Museums and art galleries	Police	Economic development (help and advice to businesses etc.)	Licensing (entertainments etc.)	Housing	Parks and open spaces	Leisure (pools, sports centres etc.)	Street cleaning	Refuse collection	Development control and local plans	Building control	Environmental health	Council tax and housing benefit	Coastal protection	Public toilets	Council tax collection
Metropolitan councils	●	●	□	●	●	●	●	●	○	●	●	●	○	●	●	●	●	●	●	●	●	●	●	●	●	●	●
London borough councils	●	●	□	●	●	●	●	●	○		●	●		●	●	●	●	●	●	●	●	●	●	●		●	●
English county councils	●	●	●	●	●	●	●	●	●	●	●	●	○	●												●	
English district councils										●	●				●	●	●	●	●	●	●	●	●	●	●	●	●
Welsh county councils	●	●		●	●	●	●	●	●	●	●	●	○	●												●	
Welsh district councils			●	×						●	●				●	●	●	●	●	●	●	●	●	●	●	●	●

Key:
- ● Council runs service on its own
- ○ May be responsible for service jointly with another council
- × Some Welsh district councils are responsible for libraries
- □ Waste disposal is run by separate waste disposal authorities in some parts of London

Information on services shown in ▓ will be published in a local newspaper from 1994.
Information on services shown in ☐ will be published in a local newspaper from 1995.
Services shown in ▓ are not yet covered by Citizen's Charter indicators.

PART 2

SPECIAL FACTORS TO TAKE INTO ACCOUNT WHEN DECIDING WHETHER YOUR COUNCIL IS DOING A GOOD JOB

In part 1, we explained how the Citizen's Charter indicators can be used to judge how well a local authority is doing its job. Local authorities need to make many decisions about the services they provide. These decisions are made by local politicians acting for the people who elected them. But in using these indicators, you should also consider how much freedom the council has over the way it runs a service. Local authorities are able to make a wide range of decisions about the type and level of services they offer. But there are circumstances, both national and local, which are outside their control and some of these may influence those decisions. You should take this into account when making comparisons between different local authorities.

How much control does the council have over the way it runs its services?

In effect, the Government now limits the money each council is able to spend. Most of the council's money comes from government grants. Each year, the Government puts aside a set amount of money for these grants. This is then divided up and shared between all local authorities, using a complicated formula which is designed to take account of local circumstances. The council also collects rates from local businesses. But this money is passed directly to the Government. The Government then divides up all the rates collected and shares this between councils according to another formula. The rest of the money the council spends is mostly raised through the council tax. But the Government now 'caps' council budgets, which has the effect of limiting the amount of council tax councils can charge.

Local authorities must provide some services by law. These are known as 'statutory services'. Local authorities can also run other services, but they do not have to provide them by law. These are known as 'non-statutory services'. But the levels of even these statutory services are not usually laid down, except for rules on particular services (for example, levels of council tax benefit). Local authorities can only run services which they have been given the powers to provide, and may not set up other businesses or commercial agencies to compete with the private sector.

Within these restrictions, local authorities can decide how they share resources between their different responsibilities, and how much council tax they charge. The way they share resources and the efficiency with which they use those resources will influence how well they do their job. For example, councils have to provide a refuse collection service, but they can decide what kinds of bins or bags they will collect and how often they will collect them. They must offer all children over five a place in school, but they can decide if they want to provide nursery schools for children under five. To get 'value for money', local authorities will aim for the best quality at the lowest cost, and higher costs should mean a better quality service. Decisions about the cost, amount and quality of services will be made by local politicians, who are responsible to local voters. Because councils never have enough money to provide all the services their residents may want, councillors have to decide which services are a priority. Exhibit 2 shows where local authorities get their money from, and how they spend it.

Exhibit 2: Local authority income and spending.

Local authority income is spent on a wide variety of services ...

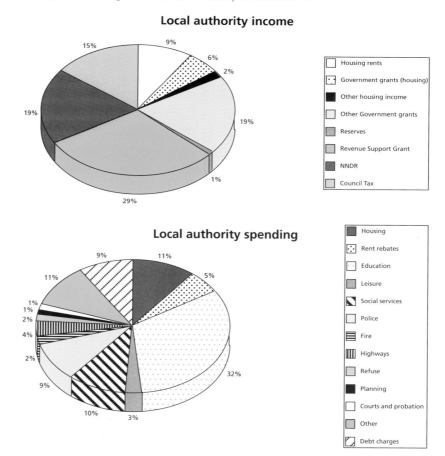

Local authority income

9%
6%
15%
2%
19%
19%
1%
29%

- Housing rents
- Government grants (housing)
- Other housing income
- Other Government grants
- Reserves
- Revenue Support Grant
- NNDR
- Council Tax

Local authority spending

9%
11%
11%
5%
1%
1%
2%
4%
32%
2%
9%
10%
3%

- Housing
- Rent rebates
- Education
- Leisure
- Social services
- Police
- Fire
- Highways
- Refuse
- Planning
- Courts and probation
- Other
- Debt charges

Source: CIPFA Finance and General Statistics 1993–4, using figures for proposed 1993/94 council budgets.

How do local circumstances influence the service you get from your council?

As well as the differences between the indicators, there are also differences between local authorities. These differences will influence the services you get. They include the area covered by the authority, its population, and its geography. Although we have tried to keep the effects of local circumstances on our indicators as small as possible, you should still take them into account when looking at performance under each one.

Some of the circumstances which influence the delivery of all local authority services are listed in the next section. This is followed by a section listing the circumstances which affect the services covered by the Citizen's Charter indicators. These lists do not include every circumstance. There may be others which you think are important and should be taken into account when looking at performance information. You may also want to find out more about your local area and whether the circumstances listed here are important. Much of the information (population density, social deprivation, ethnic minority population, age profile, and so on) is in the 1991 Census. You can get a copy of this from your local reference library.

Circumstances influencing most council services

Population density

Where people live in remote rural areas, it is harder to take services to them, or to provide services at places close to them. It will also cost more. But the problems of traffic congestion and access in urban areas will also have the same effect where local authorities deliver services directly to people's homes (for example refuse collection, meals-on-wheels).

Social deprivation

High levels of poverty and social deprivation influence the performance and cost of some services, by putting higher demands on them than in areas where there is less poverty. For example, in areas with many people on low incomes, there will be more people claiming housing benefit or needing support from social services. There is likely to be an even greater demand for services in areas with 'multiple deprivation' – for example areas with high unemployment, low incomes and a large number of single parent families. These areas are often found in the larger cities, but it is not just people in inner city areas who suffer from poverty and deprivation – they affect people in rural areas too.

Daily or seasonal fluctuations in population

Some areas may have to cope with large numbers of occasional visitors, such as tourists or commuters. This will put extra burdens on some services and mean more resources are needed than would normally be expected for an authority of similar size or population. For example, more money may be needed for policing or street sweeping.

Age of population

Local authorities with a large resident population of older people, like seaside retirement areas, will need to run suitable services to cater for this. For example, there may be a greater demand for meals-on-wheels or home helps. And in areas that have more young people and children of school or pre-school age, there may be a greater demand for youth services or nursery education.

Language and cultural differences

By law, Welsh authorities must decide what use they will make of the Welsh language in the way they provide information and services. In areas with large ethnic minority populations, especially where large numbers of people are not fluent in English, the council may give information in translation. Or they may employ multi-lingual staff with a knowledge of a local minority community. Large ethnic minority populations with different cultural needs are also likely to put extra demands and costs on services such as social services, school meals, leisure and recreational facilities.

Geographical differences

Remote rural areas will have different needs from urban areas for reasons apart from population density. The kinds of open space, highways, and other facilities that the council needs to manage and maintain will depend on where the local authority is, and what area it covers. For example, rural open space may not need as much maintenance as urban parks. But rural open space is usually more remote and harder to reach and therefore may be dearer to maintain. Bad weather will also put extra demands on services such as gritting the roads and highway repairs for frost damage. Coastal district and metropolitan councils also have to protect the coastline.

Housing and historical factors

The history of the area, its infrastructure[1], and its buildings will influence the services that are needed and how easy it is to provide them. This includes the kind of housing stock and its condition, other council buildings, private sector housing, roads, open spaces, and so on. Sometimes a council may have to live with the consequences of decisions made many years ago.

Regional pay and cost variations

In some parts of the country, especially London and the South East, council staff get extra money (sometimes called a 'weighting') that is not paid to staff doing the same job elsewhere in the country. Councils may also pay extra money in areas where it is harder to recruit certain kinds of staff. Also the cost of some materials and services which councils buy from the private sector, such as building and cleaning, may be higher in these areas due to higher wages in the private sector. These higher costs will put up the cost of running council services.

Circumstances influencing the services covered by the Citizen's Charter indicators

This section does not cover all council services, but it includes all the services covered by the Citizen's Charter indicators. The services are listed under the same headings that we have used for the indicators themselves. The indicators are listed in full in Part 3 with an explanation of the meaning of each one. This section explains how circumstances which have an effect on how a council does its job may vary between authorities.

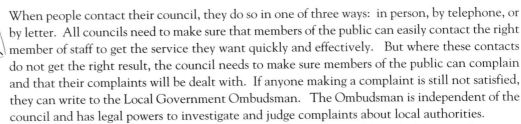

A: Dealing with the public

When people contact their council, they do so in one of three ways: in person, by telephone, or by letter. All councils need to make sure that members of the public can easily contact the right member of staff to get the service they want quickly and effectively. But where these contacts do not get the right result, the council needs to make sure members of the public can complain and that their complaints will be dealt with. If anyone making a complaint is still not satisfied, they can write to the Local Government Ombudsman. The Ombudsman is independent of the council and has legal powers to investigate and judge complaints about local authorities.

1   'Infrastructure' is the network of communication and transport services that serve a community and includes roads, railways, sewers, and power supplies.

We believe local authorities need to decide for themselves what kind of target they choose to set for answering letters and telephone calls. The council may set a target for answering within a particular time. Or it may decide to set a target for the quality of answers and check this by looking at samples of letters sent to the public or by making random test calls. Or it may decide to do both.

Complaints

The indicator on complaints is a 'check list' of good practice that can apply to any council. You can use it to judge how well your council deals with complaints. If a local complaints system is successful, the number of people who feel they need to take unresolved complaints to the Local Government Ombudsman will be low. You will need to take the size and type of authority into account when looking at the number of complaints sent to the Ombudsman – a metropolitan authority responsible for all services in its area may expect to get more complaints than a district or county council that is responsible for only some of the services.

Making buildings accessible

This section also includes an indicator on how easy it is for people with disabilities to use the services provided in council buildings. This is not just about access ramps which help people in wheelchairs to get into a building – the indicator covers a range of facilities designed to make sure the services the council provides within a building can be used by people with all kinds of disabilities. The only buildings likely to meet the full standard are those that were built recently. The performance of an authority will therefore partly depend on its programme of building new council facilities (all new public buildings must meet the full standard). Performance will also be linked to how easy it is for people to use older buildings and what resources the council has to bring these up to standard. The cost of bringing older buildings up to this standard is likely to be high.

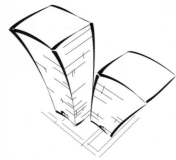

B: Provision of housing accommodation

In recent years, councils have had less of a role in providing housing because council tenants have bought their own homes under 'right to buy' schemes. The Government has also limited the money councils may use to buy or build new housing. Housing associations now take a bigger part in providing public rented housing. Many councils now arrange for tenants on their waiting list to be housed in a housing association home. A few councils have voluntarily transferred all or almost all their homes to housing associations through 'large scale voluntary transfers'. In this case, the council's tenants become housing association tenants and the Citizen's Charter indicators no longer apply to these homes. Even so, there are still around three and a half million council homes in England.

Reletting empty homes

When a property which the council manages becomes empty, the council will generally check its condition and make any minor repairs that may be necessary before a new tenant can view the property, sign up for the tenancy, and move in. If the quality of a council's housing is poor, it may delay the time it takes to relet a property. It may also mean the council has more empty properties than other authorities. Less desirable properties are usually harder to let. The high rise housing found in inner city and urban areas is generally considered less desirable than traditional housing in rural and suburban areas. Many authorities with this 'hard to let' housing have found ways to let it quickly and successfully – for example, by letting to young single people. Where the condition of council housing is poor, more properties could be empty because they are having repairs or improvements made to them, or are awaiting these repairs. A high 'capital spend' for each property should suggest that major improvement programmes are taking place.

In areas where there is a greater demand for housing, new tenants are less likely to turn down offers of a home and properties are less likely to stay empty. But some councils offer new tenants more than one property. This means the time taken to relet a property could be longer because a property may be offered to several different tenants before it is let. So the council's policy on how many properties it offers a tenant will lengthen or lessen the time a property stays empty.

Repairing council homes

Councils must keep their property in good repair except where the tenant has caused the damage deliberately. Most councils will divide repairs into 'categories' depending on their urgency, and set a suitable target time for carrying out repairs in each category. For example, loss of electrical power is a higher priority than a damaged garden fence. During 1993/94, there were no rules for what target time councils should set for each category of repair. Councils can set their own target times for 'emergency', 'urgent' or 'routine' categories. This may make it difficult to compare the information from different authorities. But from 1 April 1994, new time limits for certain repairs have been introduced. This means, by law, all councils will have to set the same target time for these repairs.

Councils may offer different kinds of appointments to tenants for carrying out repairs. An appointment which gives only the day on which a council worker will call will be easier for the council to keep than an appointment which mentions morning or afternoon, or a certain time. But it may be less suitable for the tenant.

Collecting rents

There are many circumstances to take into account when deciding how successful a council is at collecting rent. For example, although people on low incomes have a right to housing benefit to help pay their rent, they do not always claim this because they do not understand the benefits system. Or they may not be able to read well or may not speak fluent English. Financial demands and poor money management skills limit the ability of some people to pay their rent. This makes rents more difficult to collect. But councils can help to put things right by, for example, giving debt counselling and advice on how to manage money. They can also give information in minority community languages and introduce programmes to encourage the take-up of benefits. And they can make sure their debt collection service is run properly.

The cost of council housing

The cost of providing housing will be influenced by:

▲ the condition and quality of the housing stock (poor quality housing will be dearer to manage and repair);

▲ how much vandalism there is; and

▲ how often people move house (this affects how often properties become empty, as well as the amount of arrears that cannot be collected without extra cost).

Blocks of flats have heavily used shared areas that make them dearer to manage and repair. But houses have some maintenance costs (for example repairing and replacing roofs) which are likely to be higher for each home than for blocks of flats. Some homes built in the 1960s and

1970s have special problems of maintenance and poor construction that make them dearer to manage and repair.

Councils must, by law, house people who fall into certain groups. These groups include households with children, pregnant women, disabled or older people, and victims of domestic violence. They do not normally include young single people or childless couples. If councils cannot offer these people a suitable home, they may use bed and breakfast accommodation in an emergency. This is expensive and the rooms are often of poor quality and unsuitable, especially for children. Because of this, some councils have built or converted their own short-stay hostels for housing homeless people until a permanent home can be found. Some councils have also leased homes from private landlords to give people a cheaper and more comfortable temporary home.   A few councils now place homeless households directly with private landlords.

Where are homeless households housed?
The number of homeless people is much greater in inner city areas than in other areas. But housing homeless people will have an effect on any council where the demand for rented homes is greater than the supply. The council will have to put homeless people in properties which could have been offered to people on the waiting list for council housing. Or the council may have to pay to house people in temporary accommodation. But even in similar councils, performance will vary depending on how many short-stay hostels there are, and how quickly the council relets empty properties. Local policies on how many homes should be given to homeless households and how many given to people on the waiting list will also affect performance.

Local policies
Councils can declare homeless households 'intentionally homeless' where they believe these people deliberately gave up their last home. When a council does this, it does not have to house these people. Councils can also refuse to house people who do not have a 'local connection'. The rules for doing this are complicated and depend on whether people lived locally before becoming homeless or whether they have relatives in the area. These people will probably be given temporary housing while their status and need is checked. Councils will have different policies on whether homeless households need to have a local connection or whether they declare

households 'intentionally homeless'. These policies will therefore have an effect on the number of households they accept as homeless and the average length of stay in temporary accommodation.

D: Refuse collection

By law, councils must collect household rubbish. They must also collect trade waste (from shops, offices, factories and so on) if asked to do so by a local trader. But in some areas private companies also collect trade waste so the council may have to compete with them for this work. The way a council collects rubbish will depend on the service it wants to provide, and on local conditions. For example, councils may empty dustbins from the backs of properties. They may supply and collect plastic sacks. Or they may supply wheeled bins which residents leave on the pavement for collection. Councils do not have to collect garden waste or bulky rubbish, but if they do, they are allowed to charge for this service. They may decide not to charge elderly people or people with disabilities, and may also make special arrangements for these people if they have problems moving their rubbish to the pavement. The kind of service provided and its quality will affect how much it costs.

The cost of refuse collection

When rubbish is collected, it is taken to transfer stations or directly to disposal sites which may be provided by a different authority (see next section). The distance travelled by dustcarts to these sites will affect how much it costs the council to collect rubbish. There may be other circumstances which influence cost and the kind of service provided. For example, although wheeled bins are generally cheaper to empty, they may not be suitable for areas where there are steps or steeply sloping streets, or properties with no front gardens and no back entrances. In rural areas where properties are more spread out and houses are further apart, it will take longer to collect rubbish and this will mean higher costs. It may also cost more to run a service in urban areas with heavy traffic and problems getting to some properties.

Reliability

Most councils provide a reliable refuse collection service. But unexpected events, like snowfalls, can severely disrupt refuse collections. No service can ever be perfect and collections will be missed from time to time. There must be a quick and effective way of putting these mistakes right. The time it takes to put the mistake right can be affected by how far the dustcart has to travel and whether there is heavy traffic on the journey.

Recycling
Councils collect recyclable rubbish through collections at recycling centres (bottlebanks, paperbanks and so on), by separate collection of recyclable materials, or by separating refuse after collection. But they may have different recycling facilities and use different equipment. This affects the percentage of collected rubbish which they pass on to recycling companies, as well as the costs of recycling.

Free-standing recycling facilities like paperbanks and bottlebanks are cheaper to run than separate house-to-house collections of recyclable material. But councils collect less recyclable rubbish from them, especially in rural areas where people may have to travel further to find a recycling site. To get over this problem, councils in these areas may have to set up more sites, but each site may serve fewer people than a similar site in more heavily populated areas. The equipment used to separate recyclable materials after collection is expensive. So only the larger local authorities, for example, those metropolitan councils which also deal with waste disposal (see next section), are likely to choose this method. Councils can recover the cost of collecting recyclable materials by selling them to waste recycling companies. But the market for recycled materials is depressed. Recycled paper and glass are worth little or nothing so recycling can be costly. Even so, the Government has set a target for all local authorities to recycle a quarter of the rubbish they collect by the year 2000. Local authorities should recycle more rubbish to meet this target. Costs will also be affected by 'recycling credits', money paid to the collection authority by the disposal authority for materials it has recycled rather than passing them on to the disposal authority.

Reducing the amount of rubbish

Local authorities have introduced two other schemes which will have an effect on the amount of waste recycled. One is to supply containers that allow people to recycle their own household waste and turn it into compost. The other is to set up education programmes that encourage people to cut down on waste or reuse it themselves. Recycling or reuse of rubbish directly by the public is arguably the best method of recycling. But it will mean the council has less rubbish to recycle after collection and so must be taken into account when deciding whether the council has done a good job at recycling rubbish.

E: Waste disposal

Waste disposal is the process of getting rid of rubbish after the collection authority has taken it to a disposal site or a 'transfer station'. Commercial waste contractors (dealing with trade waste) also take the waste they collect to these sites. Transfer stations are used where it is a long way to the disposal site and it is cheaper to take collected rubbish to the site in bigger lorries rather than in dustcarts. A different council from the one responsible for collecting the waste usually disposes of it (see Part 1) but in some areas the same council is responsible for both collection and disposal.

Getting rid of waste

These 'disposal authorities' get rid of most waste by burying it in landfill sites. Landfill sites have to follow high technical specifications designed to make sure they are safe and do not pollute the surrounding soil or water. But with greater concerns about the environment and more local

opposition to proposed new landfill sites, other methods are being found. Disposal authorities may incinerate waste. They can make this process more efficient if the heat is used to produce electricity or to heat industrial or other premises through combined heat and power (CHP) systems. Incineration also makes the recovery and recycling of metals easier, as they can be removed easily from the ash which is left. But 85 per cent of all household rubbish, as well as all the ash from incinerators, is disposed of in landfill sites.

Recycling

The amount of waste which the disposal authority needs to get rid of can be cut even more by separating recyclable materials from it. If the council that collects the rubbish has already removed much of the recyclable material, this means there is less for the disposal authority to recycle. Most disposal authorities can also run 'civic amenity sites' where members of the public can take recyclable materials and other rubbish. But in some areas, these and similar 'recycling centres' are run by the authority that collects the rubbish. To get a full picture, you should look at the performance of the council responsible for waste disposal alongside the performance of the council responsible for rubbish collection.

The cost of waste disposal

The equipment used either to separate recyclable materials from the waste or to run CHP schemes is expensive, and the costs will be relatively higher for smaller disposal authorities handling less waste. The availability of suitable landfill sites will also affect costs. For example, a disused quarry in the area may be turned into a landfill site. Where there is no suitable site in the area, costs may be higher as the disposal authority will have to take the waste further or dispose of it in other ways.

F: Control over development

Before anyone can put up a building or make certain changes to an existing building, they usually have to ask the council in writing for permission. This is known as a planning application. You need planning permission to build or change any building except small ones like garden sheds. Also, certain kinds of development, for example where a special law has been passed to allow building to take place, do not need planning permission. The council must consider planning applications and decide whether it will allow the work to go ahead.

Deciding planning applications

The time it takes a council to decide whether to give planning permission will vary. It will depend on the type of building and the area in which it is situated. Applications for large developments like supermarkets or gravel workings take much longer to consider than applications from householders for small buildings or changes to their homes. The Government has set a target of eight weeks for councils to decide 80 per cent of all applications. This allows for the fact that councils may not be able to decide on the more complicated applications within eight weeks. We have therefore used this target as a guide for checking the speed of making decisions only on householder planning applications.

In historic 'conservation areas', like old city centres, planning applications are more complicated and will take longer to check. The consultation which must take place is also more complicated and so may take longer than in areas where the rules on planning are not as strict. Planning applications for listed buildings will also be more complicated and it may cost more to deal with them. All applications are included in the planning costs.

Appeals

Anyone who has a planning application turned down by the council can appeal to the Secretary of State for the Environment or for Wales. A large number of appeals might suggest that people putting in planning applications are not satisfied with planning decisions. If a lot of these appeals are successful, this may mean the council is making decisions which applicants think are unreasonable.

Local plans and departures

Most councils now have a 'statutory development plan' which describes what kinds of development the council will allow in different parts of its area. This is known as a 'local plan' in district councils and a 'unitary development plan' in metropolitan councils and London boroughs. The council must review this plan at least every five years after discussions with the local community. But the plan may be reviewed and updated at any time if there are changes in local circumstances and policies. In some council areas, this local plan does not yet cover the whole population. County councils also have a planning role, but the Citizen's Charter indicators do not apply to this.

When a council makes a planning decision which is not in line with its statutory development plan, this is known as a 'departure'. Departures will only happen in councils where there is already a statutory development plan. They will not be relevant for councils which do not yet have a plan. But even where there is a plan, different authorities will make their own local decisions about exactly what a departure means.

The number of departures from the plan will in part be a measure of how well the council has kept to its own planning rules. If part of the plan is out of date, the number of departures from it may be higher. Changes in local conditions and circumstances which were not clear at the time the council approved the plan may also mean a higher number of departures.

G: Payment of housing benefit and council tax benefit

Councils are responsible for paying housing benefit both to their own tenants and to private sector tenants, and for paying council tax benefit. They must also check applications for these benefits and decide how much benefit, if any, they should pay. The council may pay housing benefit to private sector tenants directly or, in some cases, to the landlord. For council tenants and for council tax benefit, payment is usually credited to the council's housing or council tax account and the claimant pays less rent or council tax. The council reclaims over 90 per cent of the money paid to council tax claimants, and housing benefit claimants who live in private rented houses, from the Department of Social Security.

Processing benefit claims

The number of claimants the council has to deal with will depend on how many people are on low incomes. It will also depend on council tax and rent levels, and how much rented housing there is in the area. Where these are higher, more people will be entitled to claim benefit. In areas where people tend to move house a lot, there will be more new benefit claims. Where there are more private landlords and more people in temporary or shared accommodation, benefit claims will be more complicated. And it will take longer to collect all the relevant information to deal with a claim. This will show up in the costs of providing the service. By law, the council has to deal with applications within 14 days wherever possible, although the way this period is measured varies with different types of benefit (see Part 3, Section G).

H: Collection of council tax

Councils have to collect council tax from all homes in their area, with a few exceptions. These exceptions include homes occupied entirely by students, newly built houses which are empty, and homes where the only occupant is in prison. Part of the council tax comes from council tax benefit. The council collects the rest by cash payments at council offices, by post, or by direct debits. The amount people have to pay is linked to the value of the property they live in. People living alone get a 25 per cent discount.

Where there is a higher turnover of households at an address, it will take more work to collect the tax. It will also be harder to collect council tax from households that have moved from the address at which they were first registered. The problems for collecting council tax are similar to those described in Section B for collecting rent. Collection rates tend to be rather lower in areas where there is more poverty. But efficient councils in these areas can show better collection rates than less efficient councils in areas where there is less poverty.

The cost of collecting council tax
Collection of tax by direct debit is by far the cheapest and best method of collection. Although it costs more to collect the tax through cash payments at local or central council offices, people who do not have bank accounts need to use this method. If a council is successful in encouraging people to pay by direct debits, this will mean their collection costs are lower. But in more deprived areas, fewer people will have bank accounts and so fewer people will be able to pay by direct debit. The costs of collection will also be linked to the numbers of people who get council tax benefit. In these cases, benefit is credited directly to the council tax account, collection is automatic and there is little cost to the council.

I: Provision of an educational service

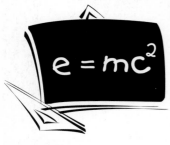

New laws have meant that school governors and headteachers have more control over their own resources. However, the education authority is still responsible for running an education service. For this reason, the Citizen's Charter indicators cover the performance of the education authority only and not the performance of individual schools. Schools are now allowed to 'opt out' of local authority control altogether. The performance of the education authority does not apply to these schools.

Within the limits of their financial resources, education authorities are free to decide what education they provide for children who are above or below school age. Many of the decisions about this are a matter of local policy. Few councils have enough funds to satisfy every demand. For example, an authority that funds places for children under five at school may have less money to use on discretionary grants for students. Some education authorities may have limited or stopped giving larger discretionary awards altogether. Instead, they may be giving smaller grants to more students.

Student grants
Many students on full-time higher education courses, such as a first degree, have the right to a grant (called a mandatory award). As long as the students and, in many cases, their parents have

given the council the information they need, an efficient authority will pay these grants by early October each year. The council can also decide to pay grants to students on other courses, but it can decide each year how much money it wants to spend on these grants.

Matching school places with pupil numbers

If local authorities try to match the supply of school places with demand, there should not be a large surplus or deficit of places – especially as the council should be able to predict the number of children needing school places. But local authorities cannot change the number of school places easily. A school may have to stay open to serve a particular community or geographical area even if it is not full. If a school closes, the council may have to pay other costs, such as the extra travelling costs to different schools. Where schools have 'opted out', the scope for making sure supply and demand can be matched will also be limited.

Local authorities do not entirely control the number of children who go to each school. Parents have the right to say which school they would prefer their children to go to. This school does not have to be in their own local authority area – many children now go to schools outside the council area where they live. Governors of some schools can set rules for taking new pupils (for example, they may give priority on religious grounds to children applying to a Church of England school). Some schools may quickly become popular, leaving empty places in less popular schools. So although a council will know how many places are needed altogether, it cannot always predict which schools will have too many or too few places.

It may take time for an authority to even out the number of places in these schools. Local people can object if a school is to be closed. They can also object to proposals for new schools or changes in character of a school such as large changes in the number of pupils. These objections are made to the Secretary of State for Education or for Wales, who will in the end decide what happens.

Children with special educational needs
Any parent or headteacher can ask the education authority to assess a child's special educational needs. These needs may be due to learning problems, or to physical or other disabilities. If necessary, the authority will write a 'statement' of these special educational needs. The authority must make sure all the educational needs covered by the statement are met. The Department for Education and the Welsh Office have set a target for local authorities to prepare draft statements within six months. This period includes time for the parent, and professionals who do not work for the authority, to take part in the assessment. The six month target takes account of the need for others to take part in assessments, although the council cannot control how quickly other people do their part of the assessment.

Because there is no agreed national definition of the kind of special needs which should cause the authority to draw up a formal statement, it is hard to make exact comparisons between authorities. Many authorities give extra help to children who have special needs but do not have formal statements. So some parents may not feel there is a need to ask for a formal statement because their child is already getting help. The number of statements an authority draws up may be lower because of this.

The law says that local authorities should educate children with special needs in ordinary schools – but they must look at each child's case on its own merits. They must also take into account what school the parents would like their child to go to.

The cost of providing education
Education spending for each pupil covers all the costs the authority has to pay, including

maintenance of schools, school meals, administration and educational services that the council (rather than the school) provides as well as the amount given to schools for each pupil. An authority can make changes to the way it runs its services. But it has less control over the type of school buildings it has to manage and the amount it needs to spend on maintenance. Spending can also be higher in areas where there are fewer people. Schools may be smaller and there will be a higher cost for each pupil than in larger schools. In these areas, the cost of getting children to school will also be higher as the distances travelled will be further. Extra money will also have to be spent in areas with large ethnic minority populations. For example, to teach English to children who speak a different first language, and to make meals that cater for special religious and minority community needs.

J: Provision of social services

Council social services departments give support to people who need help to look after themselves, for example older people or people with a physical disability, learning problems or mental health problems. Council social services departments also run children's services, for example children's homes and support to families to stop children being taken into care. These services are not covered in the Citizen's Charter indicators for 1993/94, but will be included in later years.

The wide range of social services which councils run fall into two main groups:

▲ Those which help people to go on living in the community – usually in their own homes. These services include: supplying equipment (for example, aids to help people walk); practical help in the home such as offering meals or a home help to do some cleaning and shopping; help and advice in day centres; training and help to find work; foster care for children.

▲ Residential care which, when necessary, includes care in a nursing home.

Assessing people's needs

People who ask for help from social services departments have a wide range of needs. Social workers and other professionals, such as occupational therapists, assess these needs. Assessments may be short – for example, to decide whether a client needs a simple piece of equipment or a bus pass – or they may be long and complicated. A client can be offered a range of services after a complicated assessment, from several organisations such as voluntary groups, the local council housing department and the NHS, as well as the social services department itself. Some services (for example, residential care for elderly people) may be run by private homes, but funded by the council. Private sector services may be more freely available and may be cheaper in some parts of the country. But if the council is careful when buying these services, the costs can be brought down in any area.

Care plans
New laws have been introduced to encourage the care of people needing support in their own community. Social services departments should make sure people needing help are assessed by suitable bodies and professionals. Departments must produce a care plan saying what they will do to provide these services. This includes making sure there is proper co-ordination between the different organisations providing services. Councils should encourage people who need help to have a say in their care plan when it is drawn up. Carers should also be encouraged to do this.

Local circumstances which affect how services are provided

You need to take many different circumstances into account when judging whether the council is providing social services effectively and efficiently. If many people in the area are suffering from poverty, the demand for social services will be higher. Unusually large numbers of children or elderly people (and particularly people over the age of 85) will lead to a heavy demand for social services. If there are people with specific medical or social problems – such as drug addiction – this will also add to demand. Ethnic minority communities may have special language problems and other needs. In rural areas, council staff may have to travel further to offer home care and this may put up costs. Also, facilities like day centres or lunch clubs may serve smaller populations and so can be more costly. Some of these services – for example, 'respite nights' (overnight breaks for people caring for an elderly or disabled person) – can be run by voluntary sector organisations funded by the council.

It is hard to measure how effective these services are. People who get help from them have different needs. Statistics that show how many people get help from a service do not show how well their individual needs are met. Because people's needs are different, the kind of care which a council needs to give will be tailored to each person. So social services departments have a wide range of ways of providing services. Because we are only using a small group of indicators, it is hard to measure how well all these services are working.

Good practice in social services

But it is possible to make judgements against these three basic standards of good practice:

▲ Where possible, people should be given help to live in the community rather than in residential homes, if that is their choice.

▲ Assessments should be carried out quickly. And services the client needs because of the assessment should be offered at once.

▲ There should be support for voluntary and family carers as well as services provided directly by the council to those in need.

K: Provision of a public library service

By law, councils must run a 'comprehensive and efficient' library service. They must offer books and information free of charge to people living, working or studying locally. Anyone is allowed to use reference facilities. The meaning of 'comprehensive' is not laid down, so it is up to the council to decide how much they put into the services.

Services available from libraries

One way of measuring the success of a library is by the number of books and other items the public borrows. Research shows that people in social classes A and B (people in professional and managerial jobs and their households) are more likely to use libraries to borrow books and other materials. So in a community with more people in these social classes, the library is likely to be used more. Altogether, about 65 per cent of the adult population visit a public library at least once a year.

It is harder to measure how good libraries are at offering other services. People do not visit libraries just to borrow books. In areas with many students, there will be more people visiting libraries for quiet study and a bigger demand for reference materials. Major cities need to provide wide-ranging reference facilities and business information services. Libraries are also used as cultural centres and for many other community activities.

The cost of libraries

Longer opening hours and a large number of small libraries are more convenient, but add to the cost of the service. The geography of the authority will also influence the costs and the kind of libraries the council runs. In rural communities, it may be harder for people to visit a library because they have to travel further. It will cost councils more in these areas to run libraries which are as easy to get to as they are in urban areas. Councils have to strike a balance between making it easy for people to visit libraries and the costs of running the service. One way of solving these problems is to run mobile libraries or 'book buses'. These are also used in inner city areas where fears about safety mean people, especially children, are reluctant to travel even short distances to libraries.

The amount spent on books will also depend on whether books and other materials need to be offered for a multicultural or bilingual community (including materials in Welsh). If the council decides to provide extra services like document readers for visually impaired people and computer terminals for giving out public information, this will add to the cost of the service. The condition and age of library buildings, and the money needed to maintain them, will also add to costs.

L: The maintenance of an adequate and efficient police force

The local police force is managed by a chief constable who is responsible for the running of the police in that area. The police authority, which is a committee of a county council or an authority covering more than one county or metropolitan council, decides the spending levels and chooses the chief constable (depending on Home Office approval).

Responding to 999 calls

There are great differences in the size of police forces and the kind of area they police. For example, the police will not be able to respond to 999 calls in rural areas as quickly as in other areas, because the distance from a police station or a patrol car could be 20 or 30 miles. In densely populated urban areas, distances will be much shorter but traffic congestion can cause delays.

Detecting crime

The police need to balance resources between the need to respond to emergencies, to investigate crime and to carry out other duties. If there are more officers in cars ready to respond to 999 calls, it will mean fewer bobbies on the beat. The use of civilian staff to carry out office work will also affect this balance of resources. The number of officers carrying out policing duties will therefore depend on how much paperwork is done by civilian staff.

'Violent crimes' (including murders, robberies, sexual offences and assaults) account for around five per cent of recorded crime. These crimes are more likely to be solved than crimes against property because there is often a witness (in many cases, the victim) who can identify or describe the offender. Crimes against property are much less likely to be witnessed, and so the police are less likely to solve them unless there is strong forensic evidence such as fingerprints. The number of officers working to tackle crime will in part influence the number of crimes that are solved. But the size of police forces is controlled by the Home Secretary, and chief constables must get his permission to recruit any extra officers. Within this limit, each chief constable can decide how resources are shared out between particular activities.

Crime rates are higher in certain parts of the country than in others. Detection rates also vary. More deprived areas are likely to suffer more crime. The population in inner city areas is also more changeable because people tend to move house more often. This, together with the density of the population, means that people are less likely to know the offender and be able to identify them. By contrast, in rural areas, people do not tend to move house so much, and so they usually know their neighbours and can recognise strangers. But it is becoming more common for criminals to travel long distances to commit crimes, particularly to rural areas. This is making it harder to solve crimes in these areas.

Traffic accidents

There will also be more traffic accidents in more densely populated areas or those areas with busy roads, and this will put a heavy demand on police resources. But in rural areas, accidents often lead to more serious injuries because traffic is likely to be travelling faster.

Complaints about the police

The number of complaints recorded by a police force may be linked to the number of incidents in which police officers behaved improperly. But it may also be linked to how easy it is to complain. A police force which has a complaints system which is well-publicised and easy to understand may get more complaints than a neighbouring force with more cause for complaint, but with a complaints system which is harder to use.

M: Provision of fire services

Local authorities run fire services through county council committees or through joint boards called fire and civil defence authorities in metropolitan areas. They have relatively little choice in the level of the service they provide or the way they organise it. The level of service which the authority needs to provide is mainly decided by the assessed fire risk in the area. Although the fire brigade itself carries out this assessment, it follows a set of guidelines recommended by the Home Office. The guidelines say what the minimum number of fire engines and firefighters should be to go to a fire in an area with a particular fire risk. The number of fire engines and firefighters will be higher in areas which have more 'high risk' places. The cost of running the service will also be higher.

Responding to fire calls

Under these guidelines, fire stations must be near enough to high risk places (such as large urban centres or chemical works) to allow two fire engines to arrive at any fire within five minutes of the call, and a third within eight minutes. The fire brigade must staff each of these fire engines with a crew of professional firefighters permanently on duty. In rural areas, the rule is that one fire engine should be able to arrive at any fire within 20 minutes. In this case, fire engines are often staffed by 'retained' firefighters who may have other jobs. This means the service costs less. Because journey times from fire stations to fires are usually longer in more remote areas, fire brigades may need more fire engines to respond in twenty minutes than they would need to respond in five minutes in urban areas. The Home Office also lays down rules about training and other matters to make sure each brigade is equipped to work efficiently. The easiest way to measure the performance of a brigade is to see whether it met these targets for arriving at fires. What these indicators cannot tell you is how successfully the brigade deals with fires once fire crews arrive.

Other functions of fire brigades

Although the service divides its resources to match the local fire risk, and dealing with fires is always its first priority, fire brigades have two other main functions: attending other incidents such as traffic accidents, and fire safety work.

The cost of providing a fire service

The cost of the service mainly depends on the assessed fire risk in an area, rather than local decisions or the number of fire calls. Even so, there is some local discretion in deciding what kind of service is provided and how much it costs. For example, fire brigades can decide how much fire prevention and education work they do.

PART 3

THE CITIZEN'S CHARTER INDICATORS 1993/94

This section lists all the indicators as they appear in the 'Publication of Information (Standards of Performance) Direction 1992'. This is the legal document published by the Audit Commission which sets out the indicators which local authorities must use to measure their performance. The document also sets out what information councils must publish. We have listed the indicators here exactly as they appear in the Direction. We have also added an *explanation* of what they mean and what they measure.

A. Dealing with the public

1. **Answering the telephone**

   a. The authority's target(s) for answering calls, excluding 999 calls.

   b. How performance was monitored.

   c. The performance against the target(s).

   These are all calls from or on behalf of members of the public. Authorities may set their own targets and decide how to check whether these targets are met. They can set targets for replies at the switchboard, at the extension, or both. They may set one target for the whole authority, or separate targets for different departments.

2. **Answering letters**

   a. The authority's target(s) for answering letters.

   b. How performance was monitored.

   c. The performance against the target(s).

   Authorities may set their own targets and decide how they will monitor them. The indicator covers all letters from or on behalf of members of the public, apart from letters from local councillors which

3. **Complaints to a Local Authority Ombudsman (Local Commissioner)**

   a. The number of complaints considered by an Ombudsman.

   b. The number which were classified as:

      (i) Local settlement.

      (ii) Maladministration with no injustice.

      (iii) Maladministration with injustice.

The Local Government Ombudsman is an independent official who investigates complaints made to her or him about local councils. The Ombudsman decides whether the complaint is justified – in other words whether 'maladministration' has taken place. This is what the terms used in the indicator mean:

▸ ***'Local settlement'*** *is where the council takes action to settle the complaint in a way which the Ombudsman thinks is satisfactory, without the need for a full investigation and report. In Wales, this figure includes complaints which the complainant did not follow through.*

▸ ***'Maladministration with no injustice'*** *is where the Ombudsman thinks the complaint is justified, but decides that the council's actions have not made things any worse for the complainant.*

▸ ***'Maladministration with injustice'*** *is where the Ombudsman decides that the council has made things worse for the complainant, in which case the Ombudsman will make a recommendation to the local authority about what they should do to put things right.*

4. **Handling of Complaints**

   a. The authority's definition of a complaint.

   b. The answers to these questions:

      (1) Does the authority have a written policy and procedure for dealing with complaints which covers all services and which is up to date and available to members of the public?

(2) Does it contain information on the procedure for making complaints?

(3) Does it contain a clear allocation of responsibility for receiving and investigating complaints and of overall responsibility for managing the arrangements for dealing with complaints?

(4) Does it contain time limit(s) and target(s) for dealing with complaints?

(5) Does it specify that, when time limits and targets are not met, complainants must be informed of the delays, the reasons for delay and the revised targets?

(6) Does it specify that those complaining in writing must receive a written explanation of the outcome of the complaint?

(7) Is there a follow-up procedure if the complainant is not satisfied with a response from the department to which the complaint relates?

(8) Does the authority have a written policy on remedies?

(9) Is there a system for reviewing the causes of complaints to ensure that avoidable problems do not recur?

(10) Does the authority publish a report on complaints which is available to members of the public?

Many local authorities have their own systems for dealing with complaints. The indicator shows what systems are in place and the quality of those systems, based on the Local Government Ombudsman's good practice guidelines. This is what some of the terms used in the indicator mean:

▲ 'Follow-up procedure': this allows someone outside the department complained about to investigate the complaint further. The complainant should also be told at this stage how to take up the complaint with the Local Government Ombudsman.

▲ 'Written policy on remedies': this should set out who can take action about the complaint, what arrangements are in place for making sure this happens, how the council makes sure it is acting legally in doing this, and how the council makes sure that it deals with all complaints in broadly the same way.

▲ 'System for reviewing the causes of complaints': this should include ways of recording and analysing types of complaints, and the lessons to be learned from investigations.

5. **Access to buildings**

    a.   The number of the authority's buildings open to the public.

    b.   The number of these buildings in which all public areas are accessible to disabled persons.

> This means each building occupied by the council, at least part of which is open to the public. But, it only applies to areas of the building to which the public have access. It does not include public toilets, schools and other educational buildings. 'Accessible' means that a building fully meets part M of the 1991 Building Regulations which says new public buildings must be built with a range of special facilities. These include access for people in wheelchairs, toilets for people with disabilities (where toilets are provided), induction loops for people with hearing aids, textured flooring at the top of steps and special lift buttons for blind and partially-sighted people.

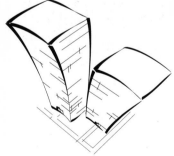

B.   Provision of housing accommodation

The housing stock

1. a.   The number of homes managed by the authority at 31 March 1994.

     b.   The number of homes adapted for elderly or disabled people.

> This indicator gives information on the numbers of homes managed by the council and the numbers in which they have fitted special equipment or which have been specially built for elderly or disabled people.

2. a.   The number of flats in blocks of three storeys or over managed by the authority at 31 March 1994.

     b.   The percentage of these flats with controlled entry.

This indicator measures the percentage of medium- and high-rise flats with all entrances controlled by staff on 24-hour duty or by entryphones in working order on 31 March 1994.

Allocations and lettings

3. The number of dwellings let to new tenants:

    a. Authority dwellings.

    b. Authority nominations to housing associations.

    and the number of these let to:

    c. Homeless households.

    d. Others.

'New tenants' here refers to tenants who are not, at the time of being housed, already tenants of the authority. To add to their own housing, many councils have agreements with local housing associations. These agreements mean councils can nominate their own waiting list, or people they have accepted as homeless, to be housed in homes run by housing associations. In some cases, housing associations may let all their accommodation in this way.

'Homeless households' means 'statutory homeless' households, which are households the council has to house by law. These are households including a person who is under 16 or over 60, a pregnant woman, a person suffering from certain kinds of long-term illness or disability, victims of domestic violence, or people who need to be rehoused in an emergency (for example because of flooding).

4. The percentage of dwellings that are empty:

    a. Available for letting or awaiting minor repairs.

    b. Others.

This indicator shows what percentage of the council's homes were empty on 31 March 1994. 'Others' means homes which the council could not let to tenants, because they were awaiting major improvements, demolition or sale, or because the council had set them aside for some other reason.

5. The average time taken to relet dwellings available for letting or awaiting minor repairs.

This indicator shows how quickly the council relets property after the last tenants have moved out. It does not include homes that are awaiting major repairs and improvements. The time is measured from the time the old tenancy is ended to the time the new tenant signs a tenancy agreement.

Repairs

6. **Response times**

    a.   The number of repairs requested by tenants at each priority level set by the authority.

    b.   The authority's target response time(s) for each priority level.

    c.   The percentage of jobs completed within target time(s).

Indicator 6a gives information to help explain the performance shown in indicators 6b and 6c. Councils must give their target times for different types of repair. Councils usually have three target response times: emergency, urgent and non-urgent, although the number of categories and the types of repair included in them may vary. Councils must publish their performance in each category against each of the targets they have set. We have not told councils how to define the point at which a repair is 'completed': is this to the satisfaction of the council or the tenant? Councils can decide this for themselves.

7. **Appointments**

    a.   The authority's policy on offering tenants appointments for repairs to be carried out.

    b.   The level of performance:

        (i)   The percentage of repair jobs for which an appointment was offered.

        (ii)   The percentage of repair jobs for which an appointment was made.

        (iii) The percentage of appointments that were kept by the authority.

Councils should say whether they have an appointments system for housing repairs, and how precise the appointments are (for example, morning, afternoon or set times). Councils do not have to offer appointments. Indicator 7b(i) shows how often the council offers an appointment to tenants; 7b(ii) shows how often tenants accepted those appointments; 7b(iii) then shows how many times the council or its contractor turned up on time.

Rent collection

8. The rent collected as a percentage of the rent due.

This means rent collected from tenants over the whole year (1993/94) as a percentage of all the rent due from all the council's tenants over that period. It includes all rent collected, including arrears which built up before the beginning of the year, prepayments for the next year, and arrears from people who are no longer council tenants. It also includes all charges made to tenants for other council housing services (for example, heating, wardens, communal facilities, and so on). But it does not include garage rents or charges made by the council and passed on to other bodies (for example, water rates). As this indicator measures collection of rent directly from tenants, it does not include rent due and paid through rent rebates (housing benefit).

9. The percentage of all tenants owing over 13 weeks rent at 31 March 1994, excluding those owing less than £250.

This indicator shows how many tenants were in arrears of more than a quarter of a year.

Costs and rents

10. The average weekly rent per dwelling.

This is the average rent on all council housing occupied as domestic homes.

11. The average weekly costs per dwelling, itemised as follows:

   a. Management

   b. Repairs

   c. Bad debts

   d. Empty properties

   e. Rent rebates

   f. Capital charges

   g. Other items, net

h.   **Less** government subsidy

i.   Total = average rent

> The figures here show spending and income for the Housing Revenue Account, an account which the council has to set up to deal with spending on council housing separately from all other spending. The costs included in the account are for both council housing and 'council housing related' buildings, which include local housing management offices, tenants' halls, estate community centres, and so on. This is what some of the terms used in the indicator mean:
>
> ▲ **'Bad debts':** the amount that the council has to allow for debts (mostly rent from tenants) which it has been unable to collect and has 'written off'.
>
> ▲ **'Empty properties':** the rent that would have been due if empty properties had been occupied.
>
> ▲ **'Rent rebates':** the council is responsible for paying a variety of benefits, including housing benefit (see Section G). For its own tenants, this is included here. The amount it must pay to each successful claimant is worked out according to a Government formula.
>
> ▲ **'Capital charges':** interest charges and repayments on loans the council has raised for building or improving council housing and 'council housing related' property.
>
> ▲ **'Government subsidy':** a specific contribution made by the Government to help the council meet housing costs including the cost of housing benefit to council tenants (rent rebates).
>
> ▲ **'Other items, net':** this includes some items of income (for example, rents on garages) as well as some items of spending (for example, rates on non-housing buildings, money transferred to capital spending accounts and used for building or improving council housing). 'Net' means the cost left over after any income has been subtracted.

12. Capital expenditure per dwelling on major repairs and improvements.

> To fund major repairs and improvements, councils are allowed to borrow money up to a limit set by the Government. They may also use money from reserves or use part of the money they raise from the sale of council housing and other assets. This is known as capital expenditure. This indicator shows the average amount spent on each home, counting all homes and not just those on which the money was spent. It also shows the amount spent on major repairs and improvements during the current year but not the amount spent on loan repayments.

C. Housing the homeless

1.   The number of households accepted by the authority as homeless at 31 March 1994, and housed in:

   a.   Bed & breakfast accommodation.

   b.   Hostel accommodation.

   c.   Other accommodation.

The meaning of 'homeless households' is explained in indicator 3, section B. When accepting people as homeless, the council may temporarily house them in bed and breakfast hotels or in specially designed hostels. Some councils also use council houses or flats which they have set aside for homeless households. Some also use housing leased from private sector landlords. Both of these count as 'other accommodation'.

2.   The average length of stay in bed and breakfast and hostel accommodation.

The average length of stay is measured to the nearest week. All households that left temporary accommodation during the year 1993/94 and were rehoused either in temporary or permanent homes must be included. This indicator also includes any time spent in bed and breakfast and hostel accommodation before 1 April 1993.

3.   The average weekly cost per household of bed and breakfast accommodation.

This is the net cost of the accommodation after income from the Department of Social Security and rents paid by homeless households are taken into account.

D. Refuse collection

1. **The service provided**

    The answers to these questions:

    a. Does the authority provide the containers for household waste?

    b. Does the authority provide wheeled bins for household waste?

    c. Is household waste collected from the back door of domestic properties?

    d. Is garden waste collected?

    e. Is garden waste collected free of charge?

    f. Are appointments given for the collection of bulky waste?

    g. Is bulky waste collected free of charge?

    h. Are recyclable materials collected separately from household waste?

    i. Is a direct dial telephone service available eight hours per working day and is there an answerphone service which takes messages of complaint at all other times?

    j. Are special arrangements made on request to help disabled people?

This check-list is designed to assess the council's refuse collection service against a standard set of factors which you can use to assess the quality of refuse collection. The meanings of some of the terms used are:

▲ *'Container' means wheeled bin, sack or anything else supplied by the council, whether permanent or disposable, to hold rubbish.*

▲ *'Provide wheeled bins' is answered 'yes' if most of households are supplied with wheeled bins.*

▲ *'Back door collection' is answered 'yes' if most households have their refuse collected from the back of the property.*

▲ *'Garden waste collections' are any collections of garden waste, whether the council allows it to be put in ordinary bins or wants it to be bagged and labelled separately.*

▲ *'Appointments' are arrangements made between the householder and the council before the day* of collection, giving the day the collection is going to take place.

- ▲ **'Bulky waste'** *is any waste that will not fit into the container that has been supplied or recommended for use by the council.*

- ▲ **'Free of charge'** *means that these collections are free to all householders, and not just free to certain groups of people.*

- ▲ **'Special arrangements for disabled people'** *means that the council will collect rubbish from a different container or from a different place than would normally be allowed.*

2. **Reliability**

    a.   The authority's target(s) for the reliability of the household waste collection service.

    b.   The performance against the target(s).

    c.   The authority's target(s) for rectifying errors.

    d.   The performance against the target(s).

In this indicator, the council should set out how it will assess reliability, what targets it has set, how it has measured whether these targets have been met, and what its performance against them is. Councils will decide how to assess reliability – for example, by the number of missed rubbish collections a week, or the number of complaints.

3. **Recycling**

    a.   The tonnes of household waste collected.

    b.   The percentage of household waste recycled.

Indicator 3a gives information to help asses the performance shown in indicator 3b. Indicator 3a means all materials collected by the authority responsible for refuse collection, whether collected from homes or recycling centres, bottlebanks, and so on. But it does not include recyclable materials collected by voluntary groups (for example, Friends of the Earth) and passed on to the council. 'Recycled' means materials collected by the council and passed on to private companies for recycling, whether by collecting recyclable materials separately from other rubbish, or by separating recyclable materials after the rubbish has been collected from homes.

4. **Expenditure**

   a. The number of households.

   b. The net cost per household.

This is an indicator of the net cost of refuse collection, after taking off income earned from any charges for special collections. The cost of collecting commercial waste is accounted for separately, but any cost or surplus from this commercial waste account is included in the domestic rubbish collection costs. This indicator covers the cost of collecting rubbish and taking it to disposal sites or transfer stations. The cost of getting rid of the waste from this point is covered in the next section.

E. Waste disposal

1. The amount of household waste received.

This is the total amount of waste the disposal authority gets for the whole of its area (which may include the areas covered by several district or borough councils, where these are not themselves disposal authorities). It includes all rubbish passed on by the council responsible for refuse collection as well as rubbish collected directly at civic amenity sites and recycling centres run by the disposal authority.

2. The percentage of household waste that was:

   a. Recycled;

   b. Incinerated with recovery of heat & power.

   c. Incinerated without the recovery of heat & power.

   d. Disposed of in other ways.

These recycling groups are counted as a percentage of the waste collected in indicator 1. As in indicator 1, recycling is all materials recycled, whether collected at sites open to the public or separated from general waste. 'Heat and power' means combined heat and power schemes where waste is incinerated and the heat used to produce electricity or to heat buildings. In 2d, 'disposed of in other ways' usually means by burying rubbish in landfill sites.

3. The net cost per tonne of household waste received.

This is worked out in a similar way to refuse collection; commercial waste is accounted for separately but costs or surpluses from the disposal of commercial waste are included.

F. Control over development

1. The number of applications for planning permission decided:

   a. Householder.

   b. Other.

This indicator gives information on the number of planning applications made to the authority and on which the authority makes a decision whether to approve the application or reject it. 'Householder applications' are any planning applications to make changes to a domestic home or its garden. They do not include change of use to a business or changes to the number of rooms in a house (for example, conversion of a house into flats).

2. **Householder applications**

   a. The authority's target(s) for dealing with householder applications.

   b. The percentage of householder applications decided within eight weeks.

The eight-week target is the Department of the Environment's recommended time for a local authority to deal with 80 per cent of all planning applications. In 2a, the council may set its own target for dealing with householder planning applications. It may also decide how to measure whether targets are being met. This could be a target percentage of applications which it intends to deal with in eight weeks, or a different time target or any other method which it thinks is suitable.

3. **Appeals**

   a. The number of decisions on planning applications taken to appeal.

   b. The number of appeals that were successful.

If a person has a planning application turned down by the council , she or he may appeal against the decision to the Secretary of State for the Environment or for Wales. The appeal will usually be heard by the Planning Inspector, an officer appointed by the Government. This indicator applies to all planning applications, not just householder applications. 'Successful' appeals are those where the inspector or the Secretary of State finds against the council and allows the development to go ahead.

4. The percentage of the authority's population covered by a unitary or local development plan.

Under the laws on planning, all metropolitan and district councils now have to produce authority-wide development plans, although some plans may not yet cover the whole local authority area. These plans describe what kinds of planning development the council should allow in each part of the council area.

5. The number of departures from the statutory plan decided by the authority.

When a council approves a planning application for a development that does not fit with its current local plan, this is called a departure. This indicator measures the total number of departures in the year 1993/94. It includes all departures and not just those larger ones which the council has to report to the Secretary of State for the Environment or for Wales.

6. The net expenditure per head of population.

This is the amount spent on processing planning applications and dealing with appeals, after taking into account the income from fees charged for planning applications. These fees are fixed by the Government.

G. Payment of housing benefit and council tax benefit

1. a. The number of new claims for council tax benefit.

    b. The percentage of such claims processed within 14 days.

Indicator 1a shows the total number of claims and 1b shows how many of these claims the council dealt with in 14 days. The 14-day target is the period laid down by the Government within which all councils are supposed to decide how much council tax benefit they will pay. The target period is counted from when the claimant has given the council all the information it needs, to when the council decides how much to pay.

2. a. The number of new claims for housing benefit tax from council tenants.

    b. The percentage of such claims processed within 14 days.

The 14-day period is again counted from when the council has all the information it needs, to when it decides how much benefit to pay.

3. a. The number of successful new claims for rent allowance.

    b. The percentage of those claims paid within 14 days.

This applies to claims for housing benefit from tenants in privately rented homes. In this case, the 14-day period is counted from the date the council gets the claim, to when it pays the money to the claimant in cash or when it posts a cheque to the claimant or landlord, or when it pays the benefit directly into an account given by the claimant.

4. a. The total number of benefit claimants.

    b. The gross cost of administration per claimant.

Indicator 4a is the total number of people who are getting each benefit, less the number who are claiming more than one benefit. This avoids double counting and shows the number who are getting at least one benefit. This figure is a 'snapshot' for 28 February 1994. Indicator 4b is the total cost of dealing with claims for these benefits divided by the number of claimants in 4a.

H. Collection of council tax

1. a.   The budgeted net yield of the council tax for the year, excluding reliefs and rebates.

    b.   The percentage of this that was received during the year.

Each year, councils work out how much council tax they are likely to collect ('the budgeted net yield') and include this in their budget for the year. This amount is usually less than the total amount which could be collected if everyone paid. It allows for an amount of non-payment due to people moving without leaving a forwarding address, refusing to pay, or other problems with collecting the tax.

It does not include: •

▲   *the council tax that the council expects to pay as council tax benefit directly into the claimant's council tax account;*

▲   *other contributions to the council tax account not collected from tax payers, such as government grants.*

2.   The net cost of collecting council tax per chargeable dwelling.

This is the cost of collecting council tax, after taking into account any income from charges made for collecting the tax. This net figure is divided by the number of homes that are supposed to pay council tax, rather than those actually paying it.

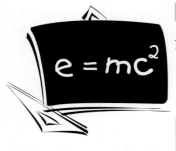

I. Provision of an educational service

Education Before Statutory School Age

1. a.   The number of children under 5 in maintained schools.

    b.   These children as a percentage of all 3- and 4-year olds.

Indicator 1a is calculated as one third of all children aged under five on school rolls on a given day in January 1993, plus two thirds of all those children on school rolls on a given day in January 1994.

Indicator 1b is taken from the Registrar-General's 'mid-year estimates'. 'Maintained' means all schools funded directly by the education authority (LEA).

2.   The cost of educating these children.

This is the total net cost after taking into account any income from fees charged to other local authorities for educating children living outside the boundary of the education authority, European Union milk subsidies, charges for school meals, and any other income paid directly to the education authority. It includes all relevant spending including the costs of teachers and administrative staff, buildings, equipment, books and educational materials, grounds maintenance, school meals, and so on.

School places and admissions

3.   The percentage of unfilled places in admission classes in:

   a.   Primary schools.

   b.   Secondary schools.

'Admission classes' are classes which children go to when they start at a school. 'Primary schools' here are those schools that accept children at the age at which they have to go to school by law. It therefore includes infants and first schools, but not nursery schools and classes. Secondary schools are the highest schools (that is, dealing with the oldest children) apart from admissions into sixth forms and post-16 classes. The percentage of unfilled places is the number of unfilled places in all primary or secondary school admissions classes as a percentage of the total number of places in these classes for each kind of school. For primary schools, this is measured at the point during the 1993/94 year (financial year not academic year) when the numbers of pupils were highest. For secondary schools, it is the numbers on a given day in January 1994.

4.   The percentage of pupils admitted in excess of schools' nominal capacity in:

   a.   Primary schools.

   b.   Secondary schools.

The definitions are the same as indicator 3. Each school has a maximum number of pupils it should accept. For the schools which have taken more than this number, these 'excess pupils' are added up and expressed as a percentage of the total number of new pupils which all admission classes in all schools should accept, for each kind of school.

Children with special educational needs

5. a.   The number of children with statements of special educational need.

    b.   The percentage of all children with statements.

This indicator shows the number of children aged 5 to 19 with statements of special needs, whether or not they are in local authority schools. If the local authority assesses the child and decides the child has no special needs, they will not draw up a statement. 'All children' in 5b means all children aged 5 to 15, no matter where and how they are educated.

6. a.   The number of statements issued during the year.

    b.   The percentage of all statements prepared within six months.

This means all statements issued during the 1993/94 financial year. Indicator 6b uses a Government guideline which says that education authorities should prepare draft statements within six months. This is measured from the point the education authority gets a written request, to the time it sends out a draft statement.

7. a.   The number of children placed by the LEA in special schools.

    b.   The percentage of all children in special schools.

'Special schools' are schools set up for children with special needs (for example, learning problems, physical disabilities, and behavioural problems). All these schools are included, whether run by the education authority or not. 'All children' means all children aged 5 to 15 whether in local authority or other types of school.

Student awards

8. a.   The number of applications for new major discretionary awards.

    b.   The percentage of such applications granted.

9. a. The number of new mandatory student awards including a maintenance grant.

    b. The percentage of such awards paid by 10th October 1993.

There are some educational courses for which education authorities must pay student grants. In many cases, this includes the payment of fees and an amount, fixed by law, for living expenses ('maintenance'). This indicator applies only to these full fees plus maintenance grants. Indicator 9b applies only to applications made by 31 August 1993. 'Paid' means posting a cheque or making payment by another method to the student's university or college by 10 October 1993.

The amount spent on education

10. The net expenditure per pupil in LEA maintained schools, as follows:

    a. Nursery & primary schools – pupils under 5.

    b. Primary schools – pupils 5 and over.

    c. Secondary schools – pupils under 16.

    d. Secondary schools – pupils 16 and over.

This applies to the net amount spent for each pupil in each category. The meaning of 'spending' is explained in indicator 2. This figure is divided by the total number of pupils in each of these categories. Some education authorities have 'first', 'middle' and 'upper' schools rather than primary and secondary schools. In this case, first schools are counted as primary, upper schools are counted as secondary. The education authority can class middle schools as either, depending on the average age of pupils in the schools.

J. Provision of social services

1. **The elderly**

    a. The number of elderly persons aged:

        (i)   65–74.

        (ii) 75 and over.

    b. The percentage of elderly persons receiving help from the authority to live in their own homes aged:

        (i)   65–74.

        (ii) 75 and over.

    c. The percentage of elderly persons supported by the authority in residential care aged:

        (i)   65–74.

        (ii) 75 and over.

The number of elderly people is taken from the registrar-general's mid-year estimates. 'Receiving help' means having a home help to help carry out day-to-day tasks. It does not include help from wardens of sheltered housing schemes. 'Supported in residential care' applies to all cases where the council gives some financial support, however small. It applies to people in homes run by this council or another council, and to people in private and voluntary sector homes. But it does not include people in sheltered housing schemes and 'part-time' care such as lunch clubs, day centres, and so on.

2. **People with learning disabilities**

    a. The number of adults under 65 known by the authority to have learning disabilities.

    b. The percentage of such persons receiving help from the authority to live in their own homes.

    c. The percentage of such persons supported by the authority in residential care.

'People with learning disabilities' are people who used to be classified as 'mentally handicapped'. The

meaning of 'receiving help' and 'supported by the authority' is the same as for indicator 1 above. 'Known to the authority' means those whom the council know about, not an estimate of the number of these people living in the area.

3. **People with physical disabilities**

    a. The number of adults under 65 known by the authority to have physical disabilities.

    b. The percentage of such persons receiving help from the authority to live in their own homes.

    c. The percentage of such persons supported by the authority in residential care.

'Physical disabilities' are disabilities or sensory impairments such as problems with sight or hearing, which make it difficult for a person to carry out day-to-day activities. It includes people who are registered disabled, but also includes others who may not be registered. The meaning of other terms is the same as in 1 and 2.

4. **People with mental health problems**

    a. The number of adults aged under 65 with mental health problems receiving help from the authority to live in their own homes.

    b. The number of such persons supported by the authority in residential care.

'People with mental health problems' are those people suffering from named mental illnesses such as schizophrenia or depression. The meaning of other terms is the same as in 1 to 3.

5. **Helping people to live at home**

    a. The total number of persons receiving help from the authority to live in their own homes.

    b. The percentage of those receiving such help who receive help from the authority on:

        (i)   2–5 visits per week

        (ii) 6 or more visits per week.

The total here may be more than the sum of the last four groups, as some other people (for example, those with long-term health problems) may also get help from the council. This indicator again applies to visits from home helps offering practical help, rather than from other social services staff. A visit of any length or at any time (day or night) is counted as one visit.

6. **Assessment for social services**

   a. The number of adults referred to the authority for assessment for the provision of social services.

   b. The number of assessments recommending:

      (i) No service.

      (ii) Service by a single agency.

      (iii) Service by more than one agency.

By law, councils must in most cases give an assessment of a person's need for support if they ask for it. They must also give an assessment if another agency or professional (for example, a doctor) asks for it. The indicator applies to all assessments made in 1993/94. After assessment, the council may recommend that no support ('no service') is needed. This includes cases where people are given only general advice but no practical help. 'Support from a single agency' means support from any one body, for example, a council or a health authority. In this case, the council counts as one agency even if a person is getting support from more than one department.

7. **Provision of equipment**

   a. The number of requests for bath board and/or bath seat.

   b. The sum of the number of bath boards and baths seats provided.

   c. The local target(s) for speed of provision.

   d. The percentage provided within target(s).

Social services departments give out many items of small equipment to make the lives of people they support easier. Examples of these are bath boards and seats. These fit on a bath and make it easier to get in and out of the bath, or can be used as a seat in the bath. There is a lot of demand for these items of equipment, and consumer groups get many complaints about how long it takes for people to get them. *Indicator 7a is the number of requests for a bath board or a bath seat. If someone asks for both items, it is counted as one request. Indicator 7b is the total number of bath seats and bath boards supplied. Councils are encouraged to set targets for the time taken to supply this equipment, but do not have to set targets. Councils may have different targets for people with different needs.*

8. The number of respite nights provided or funded by the authority.

Respite care is short-term care for people covered in indicators 1 to 4, who are normally cared for at home by someone in their household. Respite care gives carers a break. The council may offer respite care in one of its own homes or at the home of the person being cared for. This indicator applies to respite care which is provided for at least one night but less than three months, and shows the number of nights of respite care provided during 1993/94.

9. **Expenditure** The net expenditure per head of population on social services, as follows:

   a. Elderly and physical disabilities.

   b. Learning disabilities.

   c. Mental health.

This applies to the net cost of services for each person in the local authority area, not just for the people in each group. It is the total cost of providing social services in each group after taking off any fees and charges collected by the council.

K. Provision of a public library service

1. The number of items issued by the authority's libraries:

   a. Books.

   b. Other items.

'Other items' includes tapes, records and pictures, or any other items which may be borrowed from the library without charge and must be returned by a given date.

2. The number of public libraries:

    a. Open 45 hours per week or more.

    b. Open 30–44 hours per week.

    c. Open 10 to 29 hours per week.

    d. Mobile libraries.

This includes all libraries open to the public. It does not include libraries in buildings where only certain groups of people may use the library (for example, in homes for elderly people). 'Mobile libraries' include book buses and other mobile facilities designed to bring books for lending to any age group. Libraries open less than ten hours a week not included.

3. The number of visits by members of the public to public libraries.

This indicator applies to all visits by the public for whatever reason.

4. The amount spent per head of population on books & other materials.

This includes amounts spent on books, tapes, records, newspapers, book binding and other materials needed to run a library (it does not include things like tables, chairs, desks and so on).

5. The net expenditure per head of population on libraries.

This is the total amount spent on libraries for each person in the area, after taking off any money earned from fees and charges.

L. The maintenance of an adequate and efficient police force

1. **999 Calls**

   a. The number of 999 calls received.

   b. The local target time for answering 999 calls.

   c. The percentage of 999 calls answered within that target.

   This indicator means the time taken to answer the phone, not the time it takes police officers to go to an incident. Police forces must say how they carried out monitoring and exactly what they monitored. For example, most forces will only be able to monitor the time taken to reply to calls after they have first been answered and put through to them by the British Telecom emergency switchboard.

2. **Incidents needing an immediate response**

   a. The local definition of 'incidents needing an immediate response'.

   b. The number of such incidents.

   c. The local target time(s) for responding to such incidents.

   d. The percentage of responses to such incidents within the target time(s).

   Police forces must explain what they mean by an incident that needs an immediate response. 'Immediate response' includes only genuine emergencies, and therefore may not cover all 999 calls. A police force may set different targets for different areas (for example, quicker in a town, slower in a rural area). They should draw up ways of monitoring their performance and check if the targets have been met.

3. **Crime**

   a. The number of recorded crimes:

   (i) Total crimes per 1000 population.

   (ii) Violent crimes per 1000 population.

   (iii) Burglaries of dwellings per 1000 dwellings.

Total crimes are all those incidents recorded by the police, except criminal damage costing less than £20 to put right. 'Violent crime' is split into three main groups; 'violence against the person' including murder, serious assault, and causing death by dangerous driving; 'sexual offences' including rape and indecent assault; and 'robbery' which is theft from a person where violence is used or threatened.

    b.   The percentage of crimes detected by primary and by other means (reported separately):

        (i)   All crimes.

        (ii)   Violent crimes.

        (iii) Burglaries of dwellings.

This indicator is about all crimes solved. 'Primary detections' are where the police have needed to carry out more investigation to solve the crime. It includes crimes for which a person was cautioned, charged or summonsed. It includes crimes which the police knew about, and which a person asked to be taken into consideration when they were charged with another offence. It also includes crimes where the police know the identity of the offender, but decide further action is not appropriate. 'Other means' are where less investigation was needed. It includes crimes which the police did not know about, and which a person asked to be taken into account when they were charged with another offence. It also includes crimes detected when convicted offenders are interviewed in prison.

    c.   The number of crimes detected, by primary means, per officer.

The number of police officers used in this indicator and throughout indicators in this section, is the total number of police officers in the force at all ranks, except for police civilian staff, police on special duties (for example, protection of diplomats) and police officers funded by other agencies (for example, airports).

Traffic

4. a.   The number of screening breath tests administered.

    b.   The percentage of such breath tests which proved positive, or were refused by a driver.

This only applies to roadside tests of drivers for alcohol. 'Positive' means those tests where the levels of blood alcohol indicated by breath tests were more than the amount allowed by law.

5. a. The number of road traffic accidents involving death or personal injury.

   b. The percentage of such accidents in which at least one driver tested positive for alcohol.

This indicator covers all accidents recorded by the police where someone was injured, whether the victim needed hospital treatment or not.

6. **Complaints**

   a. The number of complaint cases recorded by the police force.

   b. The number of complaints recorded from or on behalf of members of the public.

   c. The number of such complaints substantiated.

   d. The number of such complaints resolved informally.

This indicator is about complaints by or for a member of the public about police officers. Indicator 6a shows the number of incidents which complaints are made about; 6b shows the total number of separate complaints against individual police officers (one complaint case in 6a may involve complaints against more than one officer or about different things linked to one incident). 'Substantiated' here means complaints where there is evidence to confirm that the complaint is true. Less serious complaints may be 'resolved informally', usually by talking to the person making the complaint.

Resources

7. The number of police officers available for ordinary duty per 1000 population.

The number of police officers is the same as used in indicator 3. 'Population' means the total number of people within the police authority area, which may cover more than one metropolitan or county council area.

8. The net expenditure on police per head of population, itemised as follows:

   a. Pay and allowances of constables.

   b. Pay and allowances of ranks above constable.

   c. Pay of civilian staff.

d.   Police pensions and superannuation contributions.

e.   Other costs.

f.   *less* Government grant.

g.   Net cost to the authority.

This indicator shows the cost of the police to the councils within the police authority area, after taking off the grant given directly to the police authority by the Government. The indicator shows the amount spent on police staff; 'other costs' includes the cost of buildings, equipment, vehicles, and so on. 'Population' again means the total number of people living in the police authority area.

M.   Provision of fire services

1.   The number of calls to:

a.   Fires (excluding false alarms).

b.   Fires (false alarms).

c.   Other incidents.

This measures the number of times a fire crew left the fire station to go to an incident. 'False alarms' are incidents where no service was supplied because there had been no fire, because the call resulted from a faulty alarm, because the caller reporting the fire was mistaken or because the call was a hoax. 'Fires' include fires which had been put out by the time the fire crew arrived. 'Other incidents' includes going to road accidents, jammed lifts, building collapses, and so on. This figure includes incidents where no service was needed (for example, where a jammed lift started working again by itself).

2.   The percentage of fire calls at which attendance standards were met.

Attendance standards cover both the number of fire engines used and the time taken to reach the incident. They normally include the number of firefighters needed, but this standard has been left out of the indicator. This indicator applies to property fires only, but includes false alarms.

3. The number of rescues by the fire brigade at:

   a. Fires.

   b. Other incidents.

This indicator measures rescues of people. 'Other incidents' is the same as used in indicator 1. Rescues at fires and other incidents where the fire brigade was called but fire crew did not carry out the rescue, are not included.

4. Net expenditure per head of population on the fire service.

This is the total amount spent after any income has been taken off. The 'population' here measures the total number of people living in the fire authority area.

N. Provision of services generally

1. Net expenditure per head of population, as follows. (Authorities need not publish information for activities for which they are not statutorily responsible).

   a. Education.

   b. Social services.

   c. Libraries & museums.

   d. Police.

   e. Fire.

   f. Highways.

   g. Public transport.

   h. Environmental health & consumer protection.

   i. Planning & economic development.

   j. Refuse collection & disposal.

k. Street cleaning.

l. Sport & recreation.

m. Housing.

n. Administration of housing benefit & council tax benefit.

o. Collection of council tax.

p. Other costs and services.

q. Capital charges.

r. Interest receipts.

s. Government grants

t. Change in reserves & balances.

u. Total.

This indicator shows the cost of supplying council services for each person living within the area of the council giving the information, after income earned by the council has been taken into account. All spending and income on council housing is left out – this is accounted for separately by housing authorities and is summarised under indicator 11, section B. Councils only have to give information on the costs of the services which they supply or are responsible, by law, for supplying. Only one council in any area will give the information on any one service, apart from those mentioned below. Here we explain in more detail what some of the services and activities cover, and who supplies them:

Libraries and museums: includes art galleries. Both county and district councils may give this information, as both may have museums, and in Wales some district councils run libraries.

Environmental health and consumer protection: in non-metropolitan areas, environmental health services are supplied by district councils, but trading standards services (part of consumer protection) are supplied by the county councils. So both councils will give information on this.

Refuse collection and disposal: in non-metropolitan areas, district councils collect the rubbish and county councils get rid of it (except in Wales, where district councils both collect and get rid of rubbish). So in England, both councils will give information on costs for their part of the work.

Sport and recreation: *includes maintenance of parks and open spaces, sports centres, swimming pools, and so on. Both county and district councils can supply these services.*

Housing: *includes spending on housing homeless people, renovation grants to people who own their own homes, and grants to housing associations. It does not include most spending on council housing, which is accounted for separately.*

Other costs and services: *includes all services not listed above, including: arts and entertainments, tourism, car parks, magistrates' courts, probation service, flood and coastal protection, tenanted and other farms, cemeteries and crematoria. Both county and district councils will give this information, depending on who supplies the service.*

Capital charges: *cost of repayments on loans taken out by the council to fund building and long-term improvements to buildings, roads and other facilities. It does not include repayments on loans for house building and improvements.*

Interest receipts: *will be registered as income rather than a cost. This is interest paid to the council on money it has lent (for example, council mortgages) and interest on money the council has invested.*

Government grants: *are central government grants paid to the council for certain services. These grants help to pay for the general running costs of those services. It does not include grants which the council passes on to other individuals or bodies (for example, some student grants). It also does not include the Revenue Support Grant and National Non-Domestic Rate (see below).*

Total: *is the amount spent 'per head of population' to be funded from three sources:*

Local taxation: *raised through the council tax or 'precept' by the council.*

Revenue Support Grant: *the money given by the Government to pay for a part of local government services. The Government fixes the amount for each council by a complicated formula linked to what the Government thinks each local authority needs to run its services; the council has no control over this amount.*

National Non-Domestic Rate (business rates or NNDR): *the tax payable on business properties. It is collected by the council that collects the council tax, but is then passed on to the Government. The Government then divides up the money collected and gives it back to all councils, using a special formula.*

2. **Council tax**   (Billing authorities only)

Net expenditure and income per chargeable dwelling, as follows:

    a.   Total expenditure by the authority.

    b.   Precepts by other authorities.

    c.   Net adjustments.

    d.   *less* Revenue Support Grant & non-domestic rates.

    e.   Gross council tax.

This shows how much of the money spent on services comes from the council tax payer, and how much comes from other sources. It is expressed as an amount 'per chargeable dwelling', which means each property that is used as a home or meant to be used as a home (that is commercial and business premises are not counted).

*'**Total expenditure**' is the total spending on all services supplied by the council after fees, charges and other income have been accounted for.*

*'**Precepts by other authorities**' is the money collected by one council for another authority. This includes the money passed on to the county council by district councils, and the money passed on to the Metropolitan Police by London boroughs. Collection authorities (district councils, metropolitan councils or London boroughs) have no control over the amount of precept that is set.*

*'**Net adjustments**' is included to make the sum balance. This will include money put in or taken out of balances (money which the council has in the bank and other investments at the end of the financial year) and an allowance for non-collection of council tax which is an extra cost for council tax payers.*

*'**Non-domestic rate**': NNDR, as explained in 1. This is the amount the Government gives back to the council, not the amount the council collects.*

*'**Gross council tax**' is the total council tax for each domestic property, averaged across all the council tax bands. It is the amount of council tax before any discounts, government grants for transitional relief, and so on, are taken off.*